PENGUIN PLAYS

CARVING A STATUE

Graham Greene was born in 1904 and educated at Berkhamsted School, where his father was the headmaster. On coming down from Balliol College, Oxford, where he published a book of verse, he worked for four years as a sub-editor on *The Times*. He established his reputation with his fourth novel, *Stamboul Train*, which he classed as an 'entertainment' in order to distinguish it from more serious work. In 1935 he made a journey across Liberia, described in *Journey Without Maps*, and on his return was appointed film critic of the *Spectator*. In 1926 he had been received into the Roman Catholic Church and was commissioned to visit Mexico in 1938 and report on the religious persecution there. As a result he wrote *The Lawless Roads* and, later, *The Power and the Glory*.

Brighton Rock was published in 1938, and in 1940 he became literary editor of the *Spectator*. The next year he undertook work for the Foreign Office and was sent out to Sierra Leone in 1941–3. One of his major post-war novels, *The Heart of the Matter*, is set in West Africa and is considered by many to be his finest book. This was followed by *The End of the Affair*, *The Quiet American*, a story set in Vietnam, *Our Man in Havana*, and *A Burnt-Out Case*. His latest novel, *The Comedians*, has recently been filmed, and in 1967 he published a collection of short stories under the title *May We Borrow Your Husband*?

In all, Graham Greene has written some thirty novels, 'entertainments', plays, children's books, travel books, and collections of essays and short stories. He was made a Companion of Honour in 1966.

GRAHAM GREENE

CARVING A STATUE

PENGUIN BOOKS

Penguin Books Ltd, Harmondsworth, Middlesex, England
Penguin Books Australia Ltd, Ringwood, Victoria, Australia

—

First published by The Bodley Head 1964
Published in Penguin Books 1972
Copyright © Graham Green, 1964

—

*Application for professional performance of the play in all parts
of the world, except the United States of America, Canada and
France should be made to:*

> Dr Jan van Loewen Ltd
> International Copyright Agency
> 81-3 Shaftesbury Avenue
> London W.1

*In the United States of America and Canada application should
be made to:*

> Monica McCall, Inc.
> 667 Madison Avenue
> New York 21

In France application should be made to:

> Bureau Littéraire D. Clairouin,
> 66 Rue de Miromesnil
> Paris 8

Made and printed in Great Britain
by C. Nicholls & Company Ltd
Set in Monotype Bembo

PREFACE

BY RONALD BRYDEN*

The Lord Chamberlain's ruling says that no representation may be made of the Christian God on a public English stage. However, as the old don knew who, surprised drying himself at Parson's Pleasure, draped his towel over his head while a puntful of ladies poled by, everyone's fairly disguised if seen only from the waist down. As the Haymarket curtain slowly rises, skirtwise, the lower portions of Deity become visible: heavy stone feet, about the size of a park bench; legs braced apart, like those of an athlete lifting a crowbar; knees still roughly blocked and indeterminate – how, as the sculptor says, do you visualise knees designed never to perform the knee's function, kneeling? The thighs, even vaguer, loom from the flies like rock outcrops, massive enough for the sculptor's son, with a magic lantern, to project photographs across one buttock; between them, the sculptor's doctor points out in lewd commiseration, lies nothing discernible. The work in progress in *Carving a Statue* is a figure of God the Father. In all the hullaballoo about sadism at the Aldwych and homosex at the Court, no one seems to have noticed that in Messrs Tennent's stately shrine of family drama another dogma of British censorship has been bent silly.

People go on complaining about the untheatricality of

*Reprinted from the *New Statesman*, 25 September 1964.

Graham Greene's excursions into the theatre. Hasn't it struck anyone that, straying in from his own field, the greatest contemporary English novelist might have something else more interesting to offer? True, like Henry James, he's too fine a narrator to squash himself successfully into the conventions of the stage. A narrative writer's central skills, the 'distancing' which is his main principle of composition, become impossible in the theatre; there can be none of the shifts, which make the excitement of a novel or film, of viewpoint, perspective, the whole frame of the plot. Greene uses the theatre like an outsider: but a good deal more intelligently, experimentally if you like, than its normal denizens.

He is fascinated and challenged by its limitations: the single-room set, for instance, in which the whole life of a household crams itself but no one ever needs to urinate or defecate. In the same way that he played with this convention in *The Living Room*, turning it into both plot and idea, he has pounced on the theatrical prohibition against depicting God and made a play of it. The result isn't 'theatre' in the ordinary sense, a vicarious experience. Like the best Shaw, Pirandello, Brecht and *Beyond the Fringe*, it's intelligence literately at play upon, above and beyond a stage.

Every joke is a miniature blasphemy, against some decorum or other. Greene has audaciously built a comedy on the largest blasphemy possible. His sculptor (a conflation, I suppose, of Epstein, Stanley Spencer and the Sutherland of the Coventry tapestry) has been working for 15 years on his huge image of paternity, collecting faces of notable fathers as possible models – he likes Landru's bearded ruthlessness,

but rejects it as too impersonal: 'He never killed a son.'
While he chips away dottily, high and invisible among his
creation's swaddling of ladders, striving to lend the divine
gaze not only the lightning which levelled Sodom but the
popular novelist's flair which hid Moses in the bulrushes,
his 15-year-old son potters solitarily in the workshop below,
fetching him tea, spam and Guinness, worrying about sex
and his O-levels. 'Father, what's the Act of Darkness?' he
calls upward. 'I wish you'd answer me, you're too damn
preoccupied.' In the circumstances, anything they say or do
is bound to wake large, comic echoes. As the boy experimentally fondles his first girl between the giant feet,
their shrouded owner lets fall one very small pebble. What
follows could be described as the father's taking the girl's
technical virginity to himself, and crucifying the son.

For those who can take it, it's rawly and gargantuanly
comic. Mostly the audience couldn't: they laughed nervously and seldom, obviously feeling got at. They were, of
course – not merely by Greene's favourite joke that no one's
so bothered by jokes about religion as the irreligious. In the
last act, the doctrinal batteries are unmasked. The father,
erecting God in his own image, has simply mirrored his
retreat from life into egoism: a power turned in upon its
own glorification. The God he has created is a huge white
elephant: the essence of fatherhood is to be needed, and
answer need with love. I suppose I felt less got at than some
because this side of Greene's theology has always seemed to
me one that the most agnostic humanist must be tempted to
share.

The one moral imperative on which he bases his religion

is the need of children: if a child is hungry it must be fed, if it cries in the night it must be answered. The villains in his work, as many of them religious as otherwise, are those who deprive children, who will not answer need. The fools are those who see the world as anything but childlike, a condition of need, inadequate. From this need he argues the necessity of God, and also his political leftism. It is not necessary to take the plunge into belief with him in order to feel the validity, the enormous compassion, of his view of the world; to share and enjoy its disabused humanity. *Carving a Statue* lacks lots of the things which make a 'good' play. Its plot is underdeveloped, its dialogue too symbol-laden for plausibility (and made more so by the playing of Ralph Richardson), its best effects, as I say, are oblique and extra-dramatic. But it brings into the theatre a wit and intelligence few playwrights would dare, and the immense generosity of a great moral writer. Our need, in the theatre as well, is too plain to sneeze at it.

Carving A Statue, produced by Peter Wood, with scenery by Desmond Heeley, was first presented at the Haymarket Theatre, London, on 17 September 1964 with the following cast:

THE FATHER, Ralph Richardson
HIS SON, Dennis Waterman
THE FIRST GIRL, Barbara Ferris
THE SECOND GIRL, Jane Birkin
Dr PARKER, Roland Culver

EPITAPH FOR A PLAY

NEVER before have I known a play like this one so torment-
ing to write or so fatiguing in production. I am glad to see
the end of it, and to that extent I am grateful to the reviewers who may have a little accelerated the end. At the
age of sixty there is no reason to work, except to earn a
living or to have 'fun'. This play was never fun and I earn
my living in another field.

All the same the faults the reviewers find in it are
curiously different from the faults I find, which are harder
faults to defend, and I may be forgiven perhaps for not
pointing them out. I was accused of over-lading the play
with symbols, but I have never cared greatly for the symbolic and I can detect no symbols in this play; sometimes
there is an association of ideas which perhaps the reviewers
mistook for the symbolic – the accurate use of words is
difficult, as I know from my own experience as a theatre
reviewer, when one writes against time.

I remember that when my film *The Third Man* had its
little hour of success a rather learned reviewer expounded its
symbolism with even less excuse in a monthly paper. The
surname of Harry Lime he connected with a passage about
the lime tree in Sir James Frazer's *Golden Bough*. The
'Christian' name of the principal character – Holly – was
obviously, he wrote, closely connected with Christmas –
paganism and Christianity were thus joined in a symbolic
dance. The truth of the matter is, I wanted for my 'villain'

a name natural and yet disagreeable, and to me 'Lime' represented the quick-lime in which murderers are said to be buried. An association of ideas, not, as the reviewer claimed, a symbol. As for Holly, my first choice of name had not met with the approval of the American 'star' who considered that the name had (by God knows what association of ideas) a homosexual ring. So I looked through an anthology of bad American verse in search of a prename, and found Holly – Thomas Holly Chivers had some renown in the nineteenth century. So much for symbols.

Other reviewers, because the word God frequently crops up, thought that my play contained that dreaded thing, 'theology'. Theology is the only form of philosophy which I enjoy reading and if one of these reviewers had ever opened a work of theology, he would have quickly realized that there was nothing theological in this play.

What is it about then? I have always believed that farce and tragedy are far more closely allied than comedy and tragedy. This play was to me a game played with the same extremes of mood as *The Complaisant Lover*. The first act is, almost completely, farce: the sculptor was based on Benjamin Robert Haydon, who was obsessed – to the sacrifice of any personal life – by the desire to do great Biblical subjects, already, even in his day, out of fashion. You cannot read the diaries of Haydon without realizing that he had a true daemon and yet he had no talent at all – surely a farcical character, though he came to a tragic end. In my story, as I intended it, the artist lost even his tragic end – no Tom Thumb was capable of shattering permanently his dream and driving him to the saving bullet. He had a greater capacity to recover than poor Haydon.   *Graham Greene*

CARVING A STATUE

CHARACTERS

The Father

His Son

The First Girl

The Second Girl

Dr Parker

SCENES

Act One. A studio in South London, 17

Act Two. Studio, six weeks later,   37

Act Three. Studio, a month later,   59

ACT ONE

*An early evening. The scene some suburb south of the Thames on
the main road to Brighton. There are moments when we are
aware of the heavy traffic outside. When the* CURTAIN RISES
*the stage is bare of scenery except for various props, which should
belong naturally to a sculptor's studio: not a very good sculptor.
Perhaps the room was once an old garage. This is not a realistic
play, and the characters would seem out of place in a built-up
set. A very tall ladder of an exaggerated height is propped up off-
centre against a rough stone block surrounded by scaffolding, both
ladder and block disappearing out of our view towards an unseen
platform (there is an arrangement of pulleys by which the head of
the statue can be lowered or raised). The foot of the block has
been carved into primitive gigantic feet that stand on a wheeled
plinth and reach the height of a stool from the floor. On a table
stands a bad plaster copy of Michelangelo's Pietà. On a wall is
pinned a reproduction of Holman Hunt's 'Light Of The World'
and a big photo of a carving by Henry Moore, one of his re-
cumbent women. Near the footlights stands a magic-lantern. A
tarpaulin can be raised across the statue to form a screen. A short
staircase right ends on a small landing and a door into the rest of
the house. On the left is the door of a tool-shed, and at the back
big doors open into a yard. A work-bench on the right.*

*There is a sound of chipping from above and small fragments of
stone fall on the stage. The figure out of sight coughs, mutters,
expectorates and sometimes lets out an oath. The time is evening.*

17

[*A* BOY *of about 15 or 16 enters carring a tray with two bottles of beer, a loaf of bread and a tin of salmon. He puts the tray on the work-bench and calls up.*]

BOY: Father! [*The chipping goes on.*] Father! I've brought your tea. I could only get brown bread. [*He drops a piece of bread on the floor.*] Oh sakes, we need a woman in the house. [*A long pause while he goes and regards the sandwiches and feels the temperature of the beer. He begins to cut sandwiches.*] Don't you think there's a chance, just a chance, you might come to marry again? Your heart's not broken, is it? It's not mother's fault she died the way she did. Mr Muggeridge has married again. For the third time. Cancer happens to one in six. I read that in the Christmas number of the *Literary Digest*. [*A long pause and then defiantly*] Father, please come down. You've been up there for nine hours. It's *Spam*, father. I'm going to eat one of the sandwiches. I'm hungry too. There was nothing but yesterday's kipper for lunch and half a hard-boiled egg.

[*This is to attract his father's attention. He is still busy with the sandwiches.*]

I'm starting now. I've got my teeth well into it. [*Pause.*] I'm chewing. I'm chewing hard.

VOICE FROM ABOVE: Don't go and eat more than your fair share. I'm hungry too.

BOY: I won't eat more than half.

VOICE: Don't you eat more than a quarter. You're only a quarter my age. If that.

BOY: I'm growing.

VOICE: So am I.

[*The ladder shakes and slowly the* FATHER *descends into sight, holding the ladder with one hand, tools in the other. A heavy figure, badly shaved. He is covered, hair, face and all, with the dust of stone. He might almost be a statue himself. He pauses about four steps from the ground and gazes up.*]

FATHER: You can see the expression of His right eye now, quite clear. He's coming. He's coming at last.

BOY: It's about time he came. I've known him all my life like that.

FATHER: If you had stayed as you were when your mother got you I would never have been landed with Him. I needed you badly as a model then. But you grew too quick. Before I had the folds of a nappy right, your mother had put you into shorts. A virgin and child would have been finished long before this.

BOY [*looking up*]: There's a wicked glint in the old fellow's eye.

FATHER: Why wouldn't there be? He made the world. [*The* FATHER *takes a sandwich and begins to eat.*] I thought you said it was Spam.

BOY: It is.

FATHER: It tastes like tinned salmon.

BOY: I suppose there was some tinned salmon mixed up with it. [*Pause.*] It's a disordered household, father.

FATHER [*looking up*]: There's no disorder here that I can see.

BOY: The place could do with a clean all the same.

FATHER: I'll never suffer a woman fussing around in my studio.

[*They both eat.*]

I suffer enough as it is – with Him.

BOY: Did you suffer when mother died?

[*The* FATHER *pours himself out a glass of beer.*]

FATHER: It was a shocking inconvenience.

BOY: But I suffered?

FATHER: You were too young to suffer. I think I'll turn to Guinness for a week or two. Carving a statue takes a lot out of a man. Remember to buy a case when you do the shopping tomorrow. [*He can't keep his eyes for long off the invisible face. He regards it while he munches a sandwich.*]

BOY: Do you know, sometimes I've wished you were an ordinary man. Then you could have explained things to me here at home. At my school the teachers talked too fast. You don't know any mathematics. Why should you? A blackboard puts the fear of death in you. Blackboard. Black book. Black night. Black deed. What's the act of darkness, father? [*He gets no answer. He moves towards the back of the stage, sandwich in hand.*] I was top in geography. I liked cities with Spanish names and rivers that die out in dotted lines . . .

FATHER [*preoccupied*]: The right eye's not quite as it should be yet. It's not easy working without a living model. You've got to have a very vivid imagination.

BOY [*pointing at the Henry Moore*]: What kind of a model did *he* have?

FATHER: He and I belong to different schools of religious art.

BOY: I wish you had come to my school just once. I used to boast about you, but nobody believed me. I needed evidence.

FATHER: At least I've got real power into the feet. I've done that. And I've got a *bit* of wickedness into His right eye ...

BOY: The boys with mothers were always a step ahead of the rest of us.

FATHER: The trouble is – He isn't only power. He isn't only wickedness ... Did He love? Didn't He love? What's love? There's the tricky question.

BOY: We loved you, mother and me.

FATHER: I can't avoid the question like Michelangelo did. [*He indicates the Pietà.*] The Son's dead. It's easy to love the dead – they cause no trouble. But they say He loved the world. They say He even loved his son. It was a queer way He showed it though.

BOY: Did I love mother, father?

FATHER: The feet are right. I defy anyone to question the feet. He's taken a strong purchase like a man with an iron bar in a circus.

BOY: They are comfortable anyway. We've been sitting on them a long time now, and we haven't got piles yet.

FATHER: The knees are an awful problem. He never knelt. His son knelt, and His son's mother knelt, but it's never recorded that He ever knelt. What would He kneel to?

BOY: He sounds rheumatic to me.

FATHER: It's an interesting point of anatomy. A knee is made to bend. If the knee never bends what kind of a knee is it? How do you represent it?

BOY: Perhaps he didn't have any knees.

FATHER: He has to have knees. He made us in His image.

Knees and other things. [*Pause.*] What a part He must have had to engender the whole world.

BOY: Heart?

FATHER: I only have to carve what shows. All the same how do you carve a contradiction? He has to be wicked and He has to be loving at the same time and He can't suffer or He wouldn't have sent His son down here to die. He wiped out the whole world except Noah without blinking one stony eyelid. The Egyptians were drowned in the Red Sea like so many Chinamen. Of course I can understand His attitude. I wouldn't exactly suffer if I broke Him up with a crowbar. I would be free of Him as He was free of His son. I suppose I'd feel a bit of waste, that's all. I've been at Him now for fifteen years. Perhaps He felt the same, after all the centuries, when the atom bombs dropped or the plagues came, and the earthquakes . . . A sense of waste, yes. But I wouldn't go so far as to say He suffered.

[*A pause while they both take more sandwiches.*]

BOY: Dr Parker said that mother suffered. I can remember listening outside the door and I heard Dr Parker say to the nurse 'She's gone. It's a good thing she's gone. She suffered terribly.' Where were you, father?

FATHER: Perhaps the knees are not required under the circumstances. Or I could put in embryo knees, like a child in the womb has embryo gills, because if all had gone well with the world, who knows? He might have knelt – in a sort of satisfaction. But it didn't work out that way.

BOY: Is unhappiness the same thing as suffering? Or is

suffering something worse? I cried. I didn't scream. Mother screamed. I was unhappy at first when they wouldn't keep me at school. I was failed in Latin. Failed in mathematics. A bad report on conduct. What exactly did they mean by conduct, father?

[*The* FATHER *fills his glass again. He holds it to the light, then drains it.*]

You might answer me. You're too damned pre-occupied.

FATHER: It's a terrible thing to have nobody anywhere who has any idea what I'm trying to do.

[*The* BOY *puts his hand out as though he would touch his* FATHER *to show sympathy, but his hand meets a sandwich on the way.*]

Take another sandwich if you are really hungry. But it's a mistake to over-eat at your age. Whatever that may be.

[*The* BOY *takes a sandwich to please his father but doesn't eat it.*]

Sometimes up that ladder I get the vertigo. The floor sways like a sea: I want to plunge, but if I plunged . . .

BOY: You'd drown?

FATHER [*with horror*]: I'd swim. [*A pause.*] Give me another sandwich. [*The sandwich is passed back.*] It *is* tinned salmon. What have you done with all the Spam?

BOY: It went.

FATHER: What do you mean *went*?

BOY: You must have eaten it.

FATHER: I don't eat a tin a day. Who told you to buy tinned salmon anyway? It's boys' food. I have to nurse my strength for work like this. I'm getting old. It was a good thing your mother left me an annuity – enough to keep the two of us.

BOY: In a year or two I could have been earning money for both of us, but it's an awful handicap when you've failed at everything. Even conduct, whatever that may be. I'd like to be a sailor. A first mate on the South American run. I wouldn't have to worry then about what's going to happen to the two of us later. Father, I do worry . . .

FATHER: Worry? [*The* FATHER *is astonished.*] We needn't worry. She left enough to keep us till I die. [*Pause.*] The biggest problem of all is that left eye of His. The right is power and wickedness. But I have to represent a bit of softness in the left. The baby Moses in the bulrushes, while all the plagues of Egypt boil in the other pupil. [*Pause.*]

BOY: The baby in the bulrushes? The best story in the Bible.

FATHER: He took such care of the child, launching him in that little boat of rushes. The small round belly with the navel like a thumb-mark in clay and the fingers clenched like snails and the tight closed eyes. When the eyes opened they saw a princess of Egypt bending down. He'd arranged it all to the last detail. [*Pause.*] A popular novelist couldn't have done better. [*He stares up the ladder.*] I've got the plagues of Egypt glaring away up there. That's certain. But what infernal chisel stroke do I use for love?

BOY: Did you love mother?

FATHER: Give me another sandwich.

BOY: You've finished them. What did she look like?

FATHER: Who?

BOY: Mother.

FATHER: Like a woman. What do you expect?

BOY [*moving towards the Henry Moore*]: Like her?

FATHER: Your mother wasn't so robust.

BOY: I can't remember anything about her. Not her eyes. Not her hair. Only a smell. My soap smells of her. Why didn't you make a statue of mother?

[*The* FATHER *doesn't answer and the* BOY *continues.*]
I saw a girl at the corner yesterday. She looked pretty. She was fair and her hair was tied in a pony-tail, and she had green eyes.

FATHER: When I've got His head done the body's going to be a big problem. I don't want swirling draperies. That's old Roman hat. He ought to be clothed in the wind and the waves with a touch of fire too. Some people would say I'm a thought too ambitious.

BOY: I went across to the girl.

FATHER: What girl?

BOY: The girl I was telling you about.

FATHER: Michelangelo was never afraid of ambition. Nor Rodin.

BOY: She ran away. I wanted to say Hullo to her. I had some chocolate with me. Fruit and nut. Why did she run away? I don't look like Dracula, do I?

FATHER: There are only three subjects proper for a sculptor. A virgin, a son, and Him. And even Michelangelo never attempted to sculpt Him. It's a terrible thing to be landed with the most difficult of the three by no fault of my own. I meant to work up to Him gradually. Beginning with the virgin.

BOY: I've never got it quite clear about virgins.

FATHER: I was going to use your mother's face. She had a sort of bewildered look as though the Angel Gabriel was at the window making rude signs. I'd examined a lot of other faces, but somehow they weren't right ... They were on the look-out, knowing too much, or else they were plain stupid.

BOY: Did you start a statue of her?

FATHER: I hadn't even time to buy the stone I needed. We were in here at the time and I was explaining some things to her. Then she put out the light and you began.

BOY: But afterwards?

FATHER: Her face was different afterwards.

BOY: The girl I saw in the street, would she be a virgin, do you suppose?

FATHER: I have a nightmare sometimes, when I've eaten cheese for dinner, that those feet may not be right after all.

[*A pause while he stands and regards them.*]

They are the feet of a man balancing an iron bar all right. But that fellow up there – He's supposed to be balancing the Universe.

BOY: It's a real problem.

FATHER: There are easy ways out if you let the stone dictate to you, but I don't believe in abstract art. I'm a realist. Like Michelangelo. [*He walks to the Holman Hunt.*] Holman Hunt was a realist too. The light of the world. What a subject! But he didn't get it even half correct. That's not the light of the world. That's lamp-

26

light on Campden Hill. He lived at Tor Villa and watched the way the light shone above the front door when Burne-Jones came to dinner. I keep it hanging there as an awful warning. I've practised with the iron bar, but I can't practise with the universe. It's a hard thing to be a realist if you have ambition. Michelangelo, Rodin and me. Nobody can deny we try to do big things.

BOY: The milkman says he's much too big – but then the milkman's not a cultivated man.

FATHER: I could have tackled the virgin and son quite easily. I knew what a virgin was. I knew what a son was – more or less. I'd have needed a couple of years perhaps. If your mother had been a bit more patient I'd have had the virgin roughed in before the trouble started, and all she had to do then was keep the baby small for long enough. I wanted to put gin in the milk, but she said gin gave the baby colic.

BOY: What's colic?

FATHER: But what kind of a model can you have for the Father? He's the real difficulty.

BOY: You're a father.

[*It isn't often the* BOY *attracts his* FATHER'S *attention. But this time he succeeds.*]

FATHER: Yes. Yes. I suppose I am. I did do a sketch of myself once in the looking-glass. But I couldn't picture Him badly shaved.

BOY: You could have shaved for once.

FATHER: Anyway I thought it might seem a bit conceited to use myself as a model. I produced you, but you aren't exactly the world.

BOY: Mother said I was to her.

FATHER: Women exaggerate. I tried some models for the Father. For example Mr Muggeridge at 27 Nell Gwyn Avenue, but he couldn't sit still for more than half an hour without a cigar in his mouth. God the Father with a cigar – it wasn't suitable. Then there was Henry Tomlinson from Elm Park Road. I was getting on well with him in charcoal – he had a kind of patient expression. Unlike Muggeridge. But then all the rumours reached me. It was said he wasn't a father at all. His wife had been carrying on for years with Mr Watkins of the Midland Bank. So I thought of trying Watkins instead, but the situation was delicate. It was then I thought of photos. That's been done before by painters. Sickert for example. He was not a man of my ambition, but you can learn from lesser men.

BOY: What exactly is a virgin, father? Of course I know more or less – but then bicycling comes into it.

FATHER: I've got a box of fathers over there. Maybe I'm getting stale and it's time to look at them again. [*He points at the table on which the magic-lantern stands. A lot of old cardboard-boxes are on a tray below the table-top.*]

BOY: Can I look at them?

FATHER: There's no interest in them for you. You aren't a sculptor. God knows what you'll ever be.

BOY: A sailor.

FATHER: You can't even tie a knot.

BOY: Oh yes I can. If I had a rope here I'd show you. I know ten different knots.

FATHER: You'd better be a hangman then, while there's

still a demand. I tried a murderer for a model once. He's there. In the biggest box. It's marked with an F. F for fathers. That's the one. There's a life-time's collection there. Light the lamp and put on the slides slowly. I want to refresh my memory. [*The* BOY *prepares the lantern.*] I've taken snaps of my friends. I've torn pictures out of the papers. I've found slides in junk shops. Perhaps I should have continued with Henry Tomlinson – but he was only one man, and one man's of little use to me. Michelangelo dissected dozens of corpses before he knew his way around. In that box I've tried to trap the *state* of being a father. In all its aspects. [*He goes and turns out the studio light.*] Put on a slide, boy.

[*An Edwardian photograph appears on the screen of a man with a big black moustache leaning over a frilly-child's cot.*]

BOY: What's his name?

FATHER: How would I know? He's one of the junk shop ones. I didn't take to him – his moustache doesn't help. Next.

[*The next slide is difficult to make out since it's upside down.*]

BOY: Sorry.

[*The* BOY *makes an effort to change it, but the* FATHER *stops him.*]

FATHER: Leave it as it is. I meant it that way. The Grand Duke of Lichtenstein. He belongs to my abstract period. You can't have anything much more abstract than royalty upside down. Next.

[*The next photo is one of Landru.*]

Now that's an interesting face. Even the beard had

possibilities. Something Assyrian in it. 'When the Assyrian came down like a wolf on the fold.'

BOY: Who was he?

FATHER: He killed a lot of women in France and burnt their bodies in a stove. He's got a wonderfully wicked glint. That gave me an idea for the right eye. But all the same he wasn't entirely satisfactory as a character. He killed a few women, but they were all strangers to him. He lacked the intimate touch. He didn't kill his son. Next slide.

[*The slide shows a man in a straw hat leaning over Brighton Pier.*]

Ah! His name was Davies and I thought I had a real find there. He *had* killed his son. Some question of insurance money and the boy was sick in any case. He was acquitted – the jury found it culpable neglect – and he took a holiday at Brighton. I tracked him down there and quite believed at last I'd found my model. The child had cried out as he lay sick – I read it all in the *News of the World* – 'Father, father, don't leave me alone,' and I thought of Eloi, Eloi, lamma sabacthani. I got him to tell me the story over the third Guinness at Henneky's bar with a piano playing. He wasn't ashamed – and that was godlike of him. He didn't suffer any more than God suffers. (The theologians deny that possibility.) I persuaded him to be photographed on Palace Pier, for here at last, I thought, was a man made in God's image. Don't worry about the straw hat – I'd have discarded it. But leaning there, looking at the to and fro of the waves and the floats bobbing from the anglers' lines and the great sun shining on the Steine, he failed me utterly. He said he was moving house because the neighbours talked. The neighbours. God doesn't move house when a whole nation dies. Put on the next slide.

BOY: But, father . . .

FATHER: They're all fathers. Next slide I said.

[*The next is a slide of a man playing cricket with his children.*]

BOY: Are those his children?

FATHER: I assume so. Junk shop again.

BOY: He's playing with them.

FATHER: A poor type. That fellow up there gave us free will. He threw us into the water, to sink or swim. It's consonant with human dignity. But that man's trying to *teach* his children. He's brain-washing them into cricket. I never made you play cricket, did I?

BOY: No. [*Pause.*] You aren't that much interested, are you?

FATHER: My time is fully occupied.

BOY: If I got sick and died . . .

FATHER: They say He likes us dead. [*The* FATHER *gets up and wipes his mouth. He stretches.*] Time to call it a day.

BOY: Last night I saw a child crying in a room across the street. He must have had a nightmare. Sometimes I have one too. Do you ever have a nightmare, father?

FATHER: He's my only nightmare, and He's there by day.

BOY: I used to be scared when I was alone in the house. When you were out looking for fathers. Sometimes I woke crying like that child. Years ago when I was young, of course.

FATHER: It's a long time since I did any research. I get nothing out of those slides now.

BOY: The door opened and a man came in. He picked the child out of bed and set him on his knee. I think he was telling a story because presently I could see them laughing. It must have been a terribly good story. Do you suppose he was the father?

FATHER: How would I know? Put away the slides. In the right order. I don't want them all mixed up.

[*The* BOY *puts on another slide. A man with a pair of binoculars half lowered, gazing hard.*]

BOY: Here's Dr Parker. Is he a father?

FATHER: There are rumours, but no real evidence. I did consider him once. His victims die often enough, like His.

BOY: Is he at the races?

FATHER: No. He's birdwatching. In every sense of the word.

[*The* BOY *puts away the slides.*]

BOY: Here's a box marked V, father. Was that when you were planning to carve a virgin? Where are you going, father?

FATHER: Out.

BOY: Can I come with you?

FATHER: No. It's my time for reflection.

BOY: Is mother's picture in the box marked V?

[*The* FATHER *finds an ancient bowler hat and puts it on, dusting it first.*]

FATHER [*turning and looking at the statue*]: Tomorrow I'll get to work on that left eye. It's a terrible problem I've set myself. Sometimes I wish I'd been to art-school like the others and learnt their facility. It's an awful thing to work out everything from the beginning for yourself.

BOY: Which is mother's picture?

FATHER: Get to bed in good time, boy. [*Pause.*] But suit yourself. It's up to you. Tomorrow remember to get the Guinness. And don't forget the Spam.

BOY: Please, father, which slide?

FATHER: What a fuss you make about nothing. There are only three slides in that box anyway. She's there, that's all I know – she's one of them.

BOY: Good night, father. I expect I'll be asleep when you get back. [*He goes out.*]

[*The* BOY *hesitates a moment and then opens the box. He takes out the slides: there are only three of them. He tries holding one of them up to the light, but the light is not sufficient. He turns on the lamp of the lantern again and turns out the light of the studio and inserts a slide. What appears is some banal reproduction from a Murillo painting – a lifeless sentimental face of a Virgin and Child. He gives a sigh, a shake of the head, and substitutes a second slide. This is a photograph of a little dead girl spread-eagled in a road – perhaps it is a blitz photograph, perhaps one from the Spanish War, perhaps from the battle of Warsaw. The* BOY *exclaims with horror and approaches the screen. He stares a long time at the picture, then kneels before it and tenderly touches the face.*]

BOY: Who are you? Are you alive? No, you're dead, aren't you? Dead as mutton. Dead as a door-nail. Dead as mother. Or are you asleep? Be asleep and I'll tell you a story, and when you wake up, you'll be happy again. I'll tell you about my father. He's big and strong and gentle too. For nine hours every day he lives up there, thinking of God and every evening he comes down here to me and we talk to each other. About everything in the world. Have you a father? He can be your father too. He's a man as high as a mountain – [*he looks up towards the head of the statue out of sight*] – with a heart as deep as a lake. Nothing bad ever comes where he is, and nothing will ever hurt you again. You'll be safe here. There are no sudden noises to frighten you, and the rushing cars are faint and far away on the road to Reigate. He'll say, 'Stay with us forever', and you'll say 'Forever' and the man as high as a mountain . . .

[*His* FATHER *comes in. He picks up the empty beer bottle.*]

BOY: Who is she, father?

FATHER: One of the junk shop ones. [*He begins to fill the beer crate.*]

FATHER: I may as well take the empties. I'm going that way. I saw Watkins on the road just now with Mrs Tomlinson and Tomlinson a while after looking patient as usual. I wouldn't be surprised if I found Muggeridge in the saloon bar smoking his big cigar. Outside the tube there was Dr Parker watching the typists coming home, carrying their little cases. The place seems to swarm with fathers of a kind today. You'd think I could get a good idea for Him and his left eye with all those fathers around.

BOY: When will you be back, father?

FATHER: I don't know.

BOY: Tonight?

FATHER: How can I tell? I told you I've got to do some research. I need a fresh idea.

BOY: What about the Spam and Guinness?

FATHER: That's your department.

BOY: I'm sorry.

FATHER: I have to be on my own when I think about Him.
　　[*He goes out. A pause.*]

BOY [*with his face close to the dead child*]: Oh sakes, sweetheart, I could do with a woman in the house.

CURTAIN

ACT TWO

*The same scene six weeks later. A sunny afternoon. The head of
the statue, which is carved from a second block of stone, has been
lowered by pulleys and stands in front of the main block. The
main block has been pulled round by a winch to make room for
it, and we now see it from another angle. Little work has been
done. The right eye is out of sight of us. The left eye has been
carved roughly out, but it's hardly an eye yet – a blank orb. One
side of the head has not been worked on at all and is nearly flat
stone. This is uppermost.*

> *[The* BOY *enters cautiously through the yard doors and
> looks around. He has a bottle of sherry under his arm and he
> carries two half-pint glasses. He puts them down by the
> statue and calls out towards the wings.]*

BOY: It's all clear.

> *[The* FIRST GIRL *enters.]*

I told you I saw him go out.

> *[The* GIRL's *hair is rumpled and wet after a bathe. She
> wears blue jeans and a shirt. A towel is slung over her
> shoulder. Her speech has picked up many Americanisms
> from the movies. She has an air of toughness, but perhaps
> she is more vulnerable and inexperienced than she appears.]*

GIRL: I'm not afraid of the old boy. I don't like scenes,
that's all. They're crummy. *[Seeing the statue.]* God
Almighty, what's this?

BOY: God Almighty.

GIRL: Where does he think he's going to put it up? In Trafalgar Square?

BOY: I never thought to ask him. It's a problem, isn't it? Perhaps there'd be room in Hyde Park. By the Albert Memorial.

[*The* GIRL *is roaming the studio. She stops at the Henry Moore photograph.*]

GIRL: Boy oh boy, did he make that one too?

BOY: No. That belongs to a different school.

GIRL: Some diaphragm she'd need.

BOY: Diaphragm?

[*She stops at the Holman Hunt.*]

GIRL: Mum had that one hanging on the wall when I was a kid. Good King Wenceslas, isn't it? [*She comes to the table where the magic lantern stands and picks up a box.*] Here's fun. What are these? Strip-tease? What does V stand for?

BOY: Virgins.

GIRL: Your Dad's got a proper dirty mind hasn't he? [*She opens the box.*] He's only got three.

BOY: One of them's my mother.

GIRL: Your mother? What a family! [*She tries to look at a slide, but there's not enough light.*]

BOY [*sharply*]: Not that one.

GIRL: Is it sexy? It looks as if she's lying down.

[*The* BOY *snatches the slide.*]

BOY: If you promise not to touch any of them I'll show you my mother.

GIRL: I don't want to see your mother. I hate family photos.

BOY: But I want you to see her. There's something very strange . . . [*He begins to prepare the lantern.*]

GIRL: If you only knew all the photos Dad shows you'd yawn your head off. Mum in Paris. Mum in Ostend. Mum's got width and you can't properly see Ostend. [*The* BOY *chooses one slide, rejecting two.*] Mum on a camel – it was only the zoo at Margate really. And colour films. Mum in Kodachrome. You can't see the sky when Mum's wearing blue.

BOY: Pull down that blind. [*He prepares the lantern.*] Over there. Just above your head. It's something very odd you're going to see now.

GIRL: You are getting me good and scared. If this is what they call an artistic family . . . They aren't vampires, are they? V for vampires. Hold my hand. [*The* BOY *gives her his left hand while he prepares the slide with the other.*] Are you a teenage werewolf – because you're sticky. Gosh, it's not human blood is it?

BOY: It's only sherry.

GIRL: We ought to have another drink before we see any horror films. It's always an X certificate for virgins. The Vampire and the Virgin. The Violated Virgin.

BOY: There's nothing to be scared of.

GIRL: The Violated Virgin Vampire.

BOY: It's my mother. That's all.

GIRL: The Daughter of the Violated Virgin Vampire.

[*The* BOY *puts on the wrong slide and the dead child appears.*]

Mercy! What's this? Did your Dad do her in?

[*The* BOY *quickly removes the slide.*]

BOY: I got the slides mixed up. You confused me.

GIRL: Are all his virgins dead ones?

[*The picture of his mother appears on the screen: a young and pretty woman with her hair in a knot above her head.*]

BOY: There.

GIRL: Is that all?

BOY: Don't you notice anything?

GIRL: No.

BOY: Look at her face.

GIRL: She's sort of pretty.

BOY: Put your hair up a moment.

GIRL: Why?

BOY: I want you to.

[*She obeys him, screwing it carelessly up.*]

There. You are the living spit of her.

GIRL: Me? You're crazy.

BOY: You can't see yourself. I can. You've got her nose and her chin. You've got her eyes.

GIRL: Make no mistake, young fellow. I'm not the mother type.

BOY: She wasn't a mother when father took that.

GIRL: Did she want to have you?

BOY: How do I know?

GIRL: Boy, if I got caught . . . Where is she now?

BOY: She died of cancer. In awful agony. In her tender twenties. Attended by Dr Parker.

GIRL: You talk as if she was someone in a book. Didn't you mind when she died?

BOY: Father says I was too young to care.

GIRL: And the old man?

BOY: He was too busy to care. You can pull the blind up now.

GIRL: Let's leave the lantern on. It's more romantic that way. With your mother watching over our revels. Come on – we'll have a drink with the old mischief maker.

[*She goes to the statue and pours out two glasses. They sit down under the head.*]

BOY: We had to lay the head down like this because we needed the ladder for the roof. The rain was dripping through the ceiling. We thought of bringing the beds down here.

GIRL: It's a pity you didn't. [*She hums a little, looking sideways at him.*]

BOY: Father said he couldn't live with him night and day. He's in one of his non-working spells and when that happens he can't bear the thought of him. He keeps away. He hasn't done a stroke of work for six weeks now.

GIRL: What does your Dad do when he stops like that?

BOY: Well – sometimes he looks at the slides – not often, because they are too familiar, and *he* sits there, father says, like a reproach. Sometimes he has a pint of bitter at the Craven Arms. That's so he can reflect a bit, he often likes to reflect. Sometimes he wanders around, looking for models.

GIRL: Girls?

BOY: No, fathers. He's been looking at fathers for nearly sixteen years now. He can't find exactly what he wants. There's always something wrong. A moustache.

41

A cigar. Too many people wear spectacles, he says, and he can't take them off because that wouldn't be realism.

GIRL: Doesn't he ever find a girl?

BOY: God Almighty's not a girl.

GIRL: I mean on a day off.

BOY: He's too much concerned with *him*. He thinks of him even when he's drinking bitter. I wouldn't be surprised if father was a genius. In his own way. Because he doesn't think about ordinary things – except sometimes he gets deadly tired of tinned salmon.

GIRL: It's a hell of a long time sixteen years to chip at a bit of stone.

BOY [*trying hesitantly a new word*]: He's – dedicated.

GIRL: Oh boy what an explosion there'd be if he quit work for a while and started thinking of girls. My sister was crazy about a sailor once – she said after three months at sea he was like fireworks and champagne. I'd have liked to know a sailor too. And all the tricks he learnt in foreign ports.

[*She takes another glass and gives him one. They drink.*]
I wish it was champagne.

BOY: I hadn't the money for champagne.

GIRL: We'll imagine it's champagne. [*She pours two more glasses. They drink.*]

BOY: It's champagne. [*He hiccups.*] You can feel the bubbles if you try.

GIRL: The old man won't come in?

BOY: He hasn't been in here for a month.

GIRL: You can kiss me if you want to.

[*He kisses inexpertly.*]

You've known no foreign ports.

BOY: No.

GIRL: You can touch me if you want. I'm safe in jeans.

[*He kisses her again, one arm round her, his hand on her thigh. She moves it up her thigh while she kisses him and then puts her own hand on his leg.*]

GIRL: You've reached Dover anyway. I bet you'd like to reach Calais.

[*She wriggles closer to him. The dialogue begins to change character – they are both a little drunk – and takes on the tones of a dream. There is no vulgarity in dreams.*]

BOY: I've been at sea a lot of years.

GIRL: How many ?

BOY: Three years or more.

GIRL: No ports in all that time ?

BOY: No ports.

GIRL: No girl ?

BOY: No girl.

GIRL: It's a long time to be at sea, that's certain. Were you unhappy at sea ?

BOY: It was all right to start with. There was the Cape of Good Hope and the sun shone on the brass work. They were cheering up in the rigging. I saw a girl with a pony-tail . . .

GIRL: I thought you said you hadn't known a port.

BOY: We didn't tie up there. I waved my hand, that's all, and she ran away in the distance. After that we lived for weeks on Spam and tinned salmon. And then came the Horn. The Horn was terrible. The wind was like a

43

bunch of razors. I thought we'd never get round Point Despair. The waves were mast high and I prayed . . .

GIRL [*slapping the stone*]: To old him?

BOY: No.

GIRL: Who to?

[*A pause.*]

BOY: I prayed to my mother.

GIRL: What did you pray?

BOY: Oh sakes, I said, we need a woman in the house. [*Pause.*] That's all I could find to pray. [*Pause.*] What's conduct?

GIRL: What we're doing now. [*She kisses him.*] Come closer and tell me more. After the Horn and Cape Despair . . .

BOY: I'm still at sea. But sometimes I long for the land.

GIRL: You can see it now can't you? [*She moves his hand a little.*]

BOY: There's a dark line on the horizon. But it might be a cloud, only a cloud.

GIRL: It's no cloud. Listen – it's the surf. It's a strange land. And I'm waiting on the quay.

BOY: I think I can see the roofs of houses.

GIRL: I can see the top of your sail, I know your ship is coming, and I can't keep still. I've got a jittery tickly feeling. [*She jumps to her feet.*] I'm walking up and down the quay from one bollard to the next.

BOY: What's a bollard?

GIRL: I don't know. Who cares?

BOY: Are there bollards in Elm Park Road?

GIRL: Don't be stupid. This is Valparaiso. I'm not in jeans.

I'm in a rose-coloured skirt, with gold shoes, and my skirt swings when I walk. When it swings men can see half way, right up to here. [*She pretends her jeans are a skirt.*] Can't you see me yet, walking on the quay? I tell you I can't stay still. If only there was a juke box somewhere. I want to twist, I want to Madison, I want to do the Hully Gully. I can see the prow of your boat now. It's pointing like a finger, pointing like something at the port. There hasn't been a ship in here for weeks, for months, it seems like years. I want to love the first man who comes ashore.

BOY: Not me?

GIRL: It will be you if you are quick enough.

BOY: Who are you? Why are you here, all dressed up like that?

[*Pause.*]

GIRL: I'm the most expensive tart in all Valparaiso. You know where Valparaiso is?

BOY: Of course. I was first in geography.

GIRL: I don't care a damn about geography. Come ashore quick.

BOY: How can I? I'm not an officer. I haven't got any money – only enough for a glass of rum and water. [*He takes more sherry and drinks.*]

GIRL: I slept last night with the governor of Valparaiso and he gave me a diamond ring. See it? [*She flashes her cheap ring at him.*] I can afford one hour for free. [*She dances in front of him, a twist without a partner.*] For free, for a whim, for an hour, for you.

BOY [*after a sullen pause*]: I don't want a tart who's

slept with the governor for a ring. I want someone to love.

GIRL: Who shall I be?

BOY: The governor's daughter. And I love you for ever and ever.

GIRL: You can keep your virgins. I'm the governor's lady. Every night I sleep in a great golden bed with a net around to stop the mosquitoes biting my velvet skin. A negro in the morning brings us coffee, but he can't see through the net where I lie naked. He can't see whether the governor's there or only a cabin-boy smelling of tar.

BOY: Where's the governor now?

GIRL: He's killing Indians in the interior. Perhaps he'll never come back.

BOY: Do you like the smell of tar?

GIRL: A-hm.

BOY: A-hm yes or a-hm no?

GIRL: A-hm yes.

BOY: Why?

GIRL: It's hot, it's strong, it's summer. I'm sick to death of toilet-water and eau de cologne and after-shave lotion. The governor uses Yardley.

BOY: But there's the smell of a port
        only the local man knows.
    Spume or tar, or even the sort
        of dung that the donkey throws.

GIRL: Where did you read that?

BOY: I made it up. We were told to write an essay on the ports of England, and I wrote that instead. They gave me zero and another bad report for conduct.

GIRL: I suppose it was the donkey did it. Why did you put in the donkey?

BOY: I don't know. He sort of walked in.

[*The dream is over. They are back in reality.*]

GIRL: Oh gosh, I'll have to be on my way. I've got a date.

BOY: Who with?

GIRL: Boy friend.

BOY: In Valparaiso?

GIRL: Stop kidding. The corner of Stanley Terrace. It's a good ten minutes away and I'm late already. [*She takes her comb out of her bag and runs it through her hair.*] Pull up the blind. I can't see to do my face.

[*The* BOY *goes reluctantly past the screen and the portrait of his mother. He hesitates there a moment looking at her.*]

Oh get a move on, do. My hair's in a tangle and I've got a smut at the end of my nose. Do you never clean the place? Doesn't your Dad notice the dirt?

BOY: He's too busy carving the statue.

[*He goes and pulls up the blind and the image on the screen fades. He goes reluctantly to the lantern and turns out the light there, withdraws the slide and puts it in the box. The* GIRL *is busy with her face.*]

GIRL: You'd better wipe your face. Your mouth's all smudged with lipstick.

BOY: Who cares?

GIRL: Your old man will notice.

BOY: Will he? I'll bet you a bob ... Shall I see you to-morrow?

GIRL: A-hm.

BOY: A-hm yes or a-hm no?

GIRL: A-hm no.

BOY: Why not?

GIRL: I've got a date.

BOY: Who's your date?

GIRL: Johnny Salt.

BOY: Do you talk about Valparaiso to him?

GIRL: Hell, no. He's not the dreamy kind. He's wild about sickles.

BOY: What's a sickle?

GIRL: Where were you brought up? A motor-bike of course.

BOY: What do you do?

GIRL: We go riding at a hundred miles an hour.

BOY: Where?

GIRL: It doesn't matter where. Into the country. Down to the sea.

BOY: And when you stop?

GIRL: We don't stop. What's the point of stopping with an Eagle Rover?

[*The* BOY *comes up and puts his arm round her from behind.*]

BOY: Do you kiss Johnny Salt?

GIRL: He's not the kissing kind.

BOY: Am I?

GIRL: I'm late.

[*The* GIRL *breaks away and in the struggle her compact drops.*]

GIRL: Damn you, leave me be. You've broken the glass. It's unlucky.

BOY: It's lucky. Kiss me again.

GIRL: I'm not in the mood.

BOY: Will you come back soon?

GIRL: How can I tell?

BOY: Wednesday?

GIRL: I've got a date Wednesday.

BOY: Who's your date?

GIRL: Joe Bridges.

[*The* BOY *tightens his arms around her.*]

BOY: Is he the kissing kind?

[*She begins to struggle away from him.*]

GIRL: Leave me be. I told you. I don't let anyone take liberties. Anyone.

[*She kicks back at him with her foot. He falls on the ground. She twists away from him.*]

Take your hand off me.

BOY: I was trying to help you. That's all.

GIRL: You can't take liberties. No one can take liberties.

[*The* FATHER *enters. He has two quart bottles, one under each arm. The* BOY *and the* GIRL *suddenly become still. They sit on the floor silent and entangled as though they hope that he will not notice them and that he will go away.*

He walks around them and deposits the two bottles by the statue. He picks up the sherry bottle, looks at it and puts it back. Then he walks into the tool-shed without a word. A pause. They are both sitting coiled up on the floor.]

GIRL [*whispering*]: Is that your old man?

BOY: Yes.

GIRL: My! He's a big man. Why didn't he speak to you?

BOY: He's thinking of the statue.

[*They neither of them attempt to get up, watching the door where he went out.*]

GIRL: Is he coming back?

BOY: I don't know. Perhaps. Perhaps not.

GIRL: Did he see us?

BOY: You can never tell.

GIRL: He looks sort of rough and hairy. Doesn't he ever shave?

BOY: Perhaps he's been at sea a long time. Like me.

GIRL: At sea? [*She looks at him with surprise. She has forgotten their make-believe.*] He's not a sailor, is he?

BOY: He's about as much a sailor as I am.

GIRL [*with withering contempt*]: You! But my! He's a big man.

BOY: I thought you said you'd got a date.

GIRL: Carving a statue like that – he must need an awful lot of muscle.

BOY: He hasn't got a sickle.

GIRL: Who's talking about sickles? [*She looks sharply at him.*] What's got into you?

BOY: I landed at Valparaiso and there was nobody on the quay.

GIRL: Are you nuts? Where's Valparaiso?

BOY: Like a fool I went into the city looking for a girl.

GIRL [*stroking the stone against which she is leaning*]: How many years did you say he'd been at it, carving this bleeding object?

BOY: They said there was the most expensive tart in the world in Valparaiso, but I only had enough for the rum and water.

GIRL: It's like a convict, isn't it, smashing stones all day?

Ten years' penal servitude and then – oh boy, the champagne and the fireworks. My sister was crazy about a convict once.

BOY: I went and looked for the governor's lady.

GIRL: For God's sake stop telling me fairy stories. What's your old man's name?

BOY [*with bitterness*]: I call him father.

[*The* FATHER *enters again and they fall silent watching him. Again he passes them apparently without seeing them. This time he picks up the beer and puts the bottles on the table with the Pietà.*]

FATHER [*paying no attention to the girl but addressing his son*]: I've got to have the head up again. I can't work at Him like this. All the piddling details – they get out of proportion. It was a mistake taking away the ladder. You go and fetch it while I fix Him.

BOY [*rising*]: It's heavy.

FATHER: You don't need to carry it. Just push it down the stairs and through the door.

BOY [*to Girl*]: You'll stay till I come back?

GIRL: I told you. I've got a date.

BOY: Meet me next Saturday?

GIRL: I can't make a date that far.

[*The* BOY *goes out.*
The FATHER *goes to the arrangement of pulleys and begins to hoist the head up.*]

GIRL: Is it heavy?

FATHER [*mockingly*]: Is it heavy? If I'd left it lying there much longer it would have sunk into the floor like a tombstone sinks in the grass.

[*When the head is dangling out of sight he gives the rope to the girl.*]

Here. Hold this rope a moment.

[*While the* GIRL *holds the head in place the* FATHER *turns the winch and revolves the main block into place under the head. While he works the* GIRL *speaks.*]

GIRL: When will it be finished?

FATHER: In a year or two.

GIRL: I bet you'll celebrate that day.

FATHER: Why should I?

GIRL: After all those years.

FATHER: It doesn't bear thinking of. What will I do when that's finished?

GIRL: Start another.

FATHER: I'm too old to start another.

GIRL: Enjoy yourself.

FATHER: How?

GIRL: Your boy brought me here. You don't mind, do you?

[*The* FATHER *takes the rope from the* GIRL *and lowers the invisible head on to the block.*]

FATHER [*looking up*]: Now I can see Him properly again with his head in the clouds. Tomorrow I'll get back to work on that left eye. Like it was when He looked at the world and loved what He'd made. At the end of the sixth day. Gentle, mild, satisfied, loving.

GIRL: Your boy wanted to make love to me.

FATHER: They double-crossed Him while He rested on the seventh day. No wonder He took a turn against the world.

GIRL [*with distrust*]: Are you an Adventist? My uncle's an Adventist.

FATHER: It's going to feel good being up there again. On my ladder. Working on the ground gives a man flat feet and a limited outlook. Tomorrow I'll climb . . .

GIRL: Like a sailor up a mast. [*She's getting restless again. She fiddles with a broom.*] A mast. A tall mast. Up a mast.

FATHER: Don't you go cleaning things. I won't have a woman in here cleaning things. Stop fiddling.

GIRL: Your boy wanted to touch me. He kissed me and touched me. Of course I was safe in jeans.

FATHER: You leave that dust alone. Carving and cooking are the same. A clean kitchen spoils the taste of food. Hygiene's like paper. It tastes of nothing.

GIRL: Aren't you angry with him?

FATHER: With who?

GIRL: Your son. He brought me in here – I was buying a packet of envelopes at Smith's, and he took me swimming at the Lido and then he lured me here and tried to make love to me.

FATHER: Where are the envelopes?

GIRL: Gosh I left them at the Lido. Aren't you angry – I mean he tried . . .

FATHER: He's too young.

GIRL: He gave me a lot of drinks. He got me tipsy.

FATHER: You aren't tipsy. You want a man, that's all.

GIRL: He touched me. It's lucky I'm in jeans.

FATHER: I did those feet before I did anything else. Sometimes I'm afraid they're the best things I've ever done or I'm ever likely to do.

GIRL: I'm telling you. It's not safe for a girl in here alone with your son.

FATHER: My son?

GIRL: He touched me.

FATHER: He wouldn't know how to begin. I thought of using him once – for the Virgin and Child. You don't have to worry about him. Get yourself a man, if you're restless.

GIRL: He says you never think about girls.

FATHER: Why should I? I've got Him.

GIRL: Don't you ever get – sort of disturbed? I mean at night – when you can't work.

FATHER: If I get disturbed I work it off.

GIRL: On him?

FATHER: One way or another. [*But she has a bit of his attention at last.*] Sometimes I get some stuff from Dr Parker.

GIRL: Who's he?

FATHER: A jovial old beast. Jovial. Jove. Jehovah. I nearly used him as a model once, but he's not a father – so far as anyone can prove.

GIRL: Is he married?

FATHER: He never found that necessary. I wrote a rhyme about him once which went the rounds and was much appreciated at the Craven Arms.

[*He circles round the girl, examining her from every angle. She stands still and lets him.*]

Botticelli

Showed the belly

And the little round tail

Through a muslin veil;

But Dr Parker
Prefers 'em starker.

GIRL: You trying to shock me?

FATHER [*with a laugh*]: You're no virgin.

GIRL: I am – sort of. Cross my heart.

FATHER: You mean you need to have the job finished?
[*He gives her a pat on the seat of her jeans.*]

GIRL: Did you ever love anyone? I mean – swoony. Like
your boy said about 'I love you for ever'. It's silly, isn't
it. But it's nice all the same.

FATHER: You want me to show you something?

GIRL: What?

FATHER: Don't complain if it scares you.

GIRL: Something you've carved?

FATHER: Something my father carved for me.

GIRL: Was he a sculptor too?

FATHER: We're all sculptors. Every one of us. He carved
in human flesh.

GIRL: Oh horrors! X certificate.

FATHER: Come over here and I'll show you. [*He moves
towards the tool-shed.*]

GIRL: I sort of like horrors. [*She looks into the wings.*]
What's in there?

FATHER: It's where I keep my tools.
[*The GIRL is scared, but she wants to follow him.*]
You can bring your bottle if you like and take another
drink to give you courage.
[*She picks up the sherry bottle and holds it like a weapon.*]
Make up your mind. If you don't want to come I'll get
back to work. Carving Him. It's time I did.

GIRL: My sister loved a monumental mason once.

[*The* FATHER *goes off with the* GIRL *following him nervously.*]

Anyway it's safe in jeans.

[*The stage for a moment is empty. From the left wing a nervous laugh. Then from yard at the back the long ladder is pushed slowly in foot by foot, like a snake. The* BOY *enters, holding the other end. He looks around the empty studio and lowers his end of the ladder.*]

BOY: Father! [*Pause.*] Father? [*He assumes that the girl has gone, but he is happy after his first real adventure.*]

BOY [*addressing statue*]: No answer of course. It's a habit fathers have. *You* would know that. I wish you'd learn to answer. If you are ever stuck up in a cathedral people will always be praying to you. For sun, for rain, for harvest. If there are enough prayers some will be answered. It's the law of averages. I got the jackpot once in a fruit machine. I can hear the music of the tanners now cascading on the floor. Send me another jackpot. Let me see her again next Saturday walking along the quay in Valparaiso. She'll say 'I love you for ever. I won't die or run away. I need you more than Spam or Double Diamond' and I'll say 'I want to give to you. I want to give everything I've got.' [*Pause.*] When I kissed her it was like ice breaking when you tread in the gutter in January. It was like the season changing, a part of you lifts slowly like a branch when the snow begins to slide off it to the ground.

[*The* GIRL *comes in from the left. She looks bemused and tousled. She is without her blue jeans. Her shirt comes*] *down to her knees. She walks by the boy, paying him no attention at all.*

When she reaches the centre of the stage the GIRL *stops. The* BOY *watches her with dismay.*]

GIRL: Where's my jeans?

[*The* FATHER *comes for a moment to the door of the tool-shed and tosses the jeans to her.*]

Where's the bathroom?

FATHER: I told you. On the left at the end of the passage.

[*The* FATHER *goes back into the tool-shed. The* GIRL *goes out, trailing the jeans after her. The* BOY *watches her go then cries to his* FATHER.]

BOY: You think you are strong, don't you? 'My, he's a big man.' You needn't feel so proud. She's only a little tart. I saw through her all the time.

[*The* BOY *collapses in tears with his face pressed against the statue. The* FATHER *enters dressed for sculpting. He is completely oblivious of his son.*]

FATHER: Here. Help me with this ladder. I'm ready for a bit of work now.

BOY: Put up your own bloody ladder.

FATHER: I've got an idea about his left eye. What are you waiting for? I want to get the ladder up quick. I'm going to start right away. I'm in the mood. I've been on the ground too long. [*The ladder is raised between them and the* FATHER *mounts a few steps. He is in a state of excitement when for once he is prepared to explain a little to his son. He turns and addresses him from a few steps up the ladder.*] You wouldn't understand what it feels like when an idea strikes you. I feel giddy with it. It's like vertigo. Hold the ladder steady or I'll fall. It's like God Almighty on the first day. When He divided the light from the dark. You can't rest till you've made the first start, and anything may follow after that. I bet He never thought of water when He made the light, and He had no idea for tigers when He made the first fish. A flat fish, it was, like a plaice, moving like a mathematical symbol, silent in the water, and then suddenly the panther, silent, undulating through the trees. I've been knocking my head against a brick wall over that left eye. But now I know. I don't have to worry about love. God doesn't love. He communicates, that's all. He's an artist. He doesn't love.

BOY: Did He hate his son?

FATHER: He didn't love or hate him. He used him as a subject. That's what the Son was for.

[*The* FATHER *begins to climb the ladder as the*

CURTAIN FALLS]

ACT THREE

The same scene about a month later. Afternoon. The BOY *is reading to the* SECOND GIRL *under the statue.*

BOY: This is the world's greatest poet. His name is Joseph Whitaker, and he has been writing poems like this for ninety-six years. You can read him while I'm gone.

    [*He sits beside her and taking the book reads aloud while she follows the text with her eyes.*]

'The marriage must be solemnized between the hours of 8 a.m. and 6 p.m. with open doors in the presence of a Superintendent Registrar and a Registrar of the Registration District of that Superintendent Registrar. The parties must make the following declaration. I do solemnly declare that I know not of any lawful impediment why I, AB, may not be joined in matrimony to CD.' I love CD because she is – because she's Calm and Dear.

    [*They kiss. The* BOY *indicates another passage.*]

Hell! Here's a piece called Minors. 'Persons under twenty years of age are generally required to obtain the consent of certain persons.' [*A clock strikes.*] I'm late. I must be off.

    [*He kisses her again and leaves the studio by the yard doors, waving to her before he goes. She puts her fingers to her lips and reads on.*

Outside there is a crash and an oath. She retreats towards the wall, where she stands in shadow behind the statue. An elderly too-dapper man wearing a dark formal hat and a dark formal suit carrying a dark formal brief-case hops on to the stage from the right – Dr PARKER. *He puts his leg gingerly down.*]

Dr PARKER: You ought to get that lino repaired. [*He feels his knee-cap.*] There's nothing like hitting the knee-cap to convince a man that he exists. [*He hops down the stairs to the foot of the ladder and stares up.*] You're the lucky one. No knees at all. Perhaps not so lucky. You lack more essential features too. You think me lacking in respect, but you are not in a church yet. Talking aloud to myself? I'm quite aware of the fact. I do it quite deliberately. Why should it be thought eccentric to talk to oneself? It's an enormous relief after talking to less intelligent people all day. My first appointment was at nine-thirty and except for lunch-time I have not been alone since then for two minutes. As for lunch-time I can hardly talk to myself at meals or I should never finish the meal. So at lunch I listened only, to my unspoken thoughts. That's no relief at all. I am a listener all day as it is, God pity me. [*He looks up at the statue.*] If you'll excuse the expression. [*He sits down on the statue's feet. He pulls up his trouser-leg and examines his knee with his fingers.*] The patella is quite undamaged. Apply a little Elliman's Embrocation, the strong veterinary variety, rubbing it gently in after warming the bottle. However now that I have you here – at my mercy ha ha – let's make a more complete examination. After the age of sixty-five one should be examined regularly. As a precaution only. No cause for alarm. You are obviously in perfect health. [*Leaving his trouser-leg still tucked above his knee he opens his brief-case and pulls out the rubber band used for testing blood pressure.*] Supposed to be the latest model. Of course the Japs are ahead of us as always. Ugly little brutes. But inventive. You can't deny that. Those 'lonely bachelor' boxes they used to sell at Kyoto. [*He pulls up his sleeve and wraps the band round his arm. Then he blows it up and checks the pulse beat with his watch.*] 110. Not bad for a man of my age – a little low, perhaps, but a fault on the right side. I wouldn't hesitate to let myself know at once if it were otherwise. What a joy it is to treat a patient without having to employ a bedside manner. I have the courage to tell myself the truth. [*He rolls up the apparatus and puts it back in the brief-case. Absent-mindedly he leaves his left sleeve rolled up as well as his right trouser-leg.*] A bedside manner is a thing that slowly, inevitably, destroys a man. A doctor may be clever, charming, assiduous, he may be loved by his patients, but he belongs to a world of fantasy. After telling a lot of frightened patients a lot of reassuring stories I find it hard to believe in my own reality. I tell little jokes – what is the difference between an elephant and a flea ? – as I feel the cruel tumour under my fingers. [*He pats the statue.*] My friend, I become like you, a block of stone, indifferent to human suffering. The thought of you soothes the dying. Just so they wait for my footsteps. Like you I offer false comfort. What other use have you ? Can you tell the difference between an elephant and a flea ? Can you tell me that ? I ask you –

and you don't answer. I implore you ... This comedy
has got to end or I shall turn serious.

[*During the last part of this dialogue the* SECOND GIRL
*has emerged a little way from the background, staring at the
doctor. He looks round and sees her. He is not at all
disconcerted.*]

DR PARKER: Good afternoon, my dear. My name is
Dr Parker. And who may you be?

[*She makes no reply.*]

I'm just waiting here for our great sculptor. Talking
away to myself as is my harmless habit.

[*She stays silent.*]

My clothes are somewhat disarrayed, I know. But for a
perfectly good reason. I have been treating myself. [*He
pulls down his sleeve, but forgets his trouser-leg.*] There's no
other doctor around here that I would trust with a
common cold. [*Pause.*] You're rather a silent child,
though a very charming one. You might at least bring
yourself to say R. [*He raps out a command.*] Say R.
[*She says nothing.*] I might be talking to the deaf. [*He
shouts at her.*] Are you deaf? [*No reply.*] Are you
dumb?

[*The* FATHER *enters.*]

FATHER: She's deaf *and* dumb.

DR PARKER: Who is she?

FATHER: My son found her.

DR PARKER: Where?

FATHER: On the Inner Circle. She was lost, I think.

DR PARKER: Poor child, defeated as we all are by the
Metropolitan system. [*He can't keep his eyes off her.*] She's

beautiful. Quite beautiful. Turn round, my dear. Oh, I forgot.

[*He crooks his finger and she approaches. He puts his hand on her shoulder and turns her around, examining her figure with an experienced eye.*]

A little Botticelli. I can see her rising from the sea in something silky and diaphanous, through which the pearly skin gleams like an oyster-shell. And what a gift of silence.

FATHER: A gift?

Dr PARKER: Oh, perhaps it was odd of your son at his age to pick on someone deaf and dumb, but for me it would have been natural. I long for the restfulness of the uncommunicative. With this child I would be forced to exchange words only at essential moments.

FATHER: And then she wouldn't hear you.

Dr PARKER: Oh yes, she would. I know the alphabet.

[*He communicates with his hands. The* GIRL *smiles and turns shyly away.*]

FATHER: What did you say to her?

Dr PARKER: I told her that her eyes are very lovely. So they are.

FATHER: Was this an essential moment?

Dr PARKER: She pleases me, my dear fellow. So one has to make a beginning with a little compliment. I wonder how your son manages to amuse her?

FATHER: They go out together – I don't know where. It's no business of mine.

[*Dr* PARKER's *eyes follow the girl who sits on the floor and looks out into the wings, waiting patiently for the boy.*]

Dr PARKER [*wetting his lips*]: Do you suppose the friendship's ripened?

FATHER: Parker, I asked you to look in because I'm frightened.

Dr PARKER: Oh well, that's nothing strange. You've reached the age of fear. I'm frightened myself sometimes.

FATHER: What frightens *you*?

Dr PARKER: The thought that I shall one day lose my physical attraction for women. [*He stretches out his legs to regard them and remembers that his trouser is turned up. He begins to roll it down.*] That nature will live on in me, hungry and unsatisfied. That I shall be driven in the last resort to unprofessional conduct with the aid of an anaesthetic. [*He makes signs with his hands to the girl.*]

FATHER: Are you telling her your fears?

Dr PARKER: Good gracious no! I'm reassuring her, that's all.

FATHER: It's me you've come to see.

Dr PARKER: What reassurance do *you* need?

FATHER: When I climb up that ladder now I always get the vertigo.

Dr PARKER: You've had it often before.

FATHER: But it's been bad lately, Parker. Now I can hardly stand up to work. My head reels. The floor below crinkles like a moving staircase.

Dr PARKER: I warned you a month ago your blood pressure was too high. It's natural at your age. With your temperament.

FATHER: But I've given up beer altogether. I don't go any

longer to the Craven Arms. I've not one pleasure left. I work, that's all.

DR PARKER: If I remember rightly your last serious attack was after a little – pleasure.

FATHER: I only had the girl once. She was a slut. I wouldn't let her in the house again.

DR PARKER: You haven't by any chance been playing around with this sweet little Botticelli here?

FATHER: She's my son's girl, not mine.

DR PARKER: So was the other, if I remember right.

FATHER: Doctor, I only need a few more months to finish Him.

DR PARKER: After fifteen years? You'll never finish him.

FATHER: You think I'm slow. Did you never hear of Sir Thomas Lawrence who was painting an earl's wife and baby. The earl wanted the picture back, but Lawrence said he hadn't quite finished. He was nearly satisfied with the countess, but the baby needed another sitting or two. 'You can have my wife,' said the earl, 'but the baby's in the Guards now.'

DR PARKER [*laughing*]: A good story!

FATHER: It's not a laughing matter. Art's stationary. It's a terrifying thing for a conscientious workman like me to watch how quickly his subjects change. Do you think even He kept up with his creation? Before He could turn round beautiful Adam became the unbearable old Israelite Abraham.

DR PARKER: I remember when you began him. Your son was ill. Remember? He wasn't yet three.

FATHER: A childish ailment – I can't remember them all.

DR PARKER: This wasn't one of those. I feared meningitis. You hid yourself down here out of earshot with your block of stone. I believe you slept with it. I call that shocking conduct. What makes you such a selfish old bastard? I've known you for twenty years and you've never faced pain yet.

FATHER: I don't know what you mean. You wait until I've finished Him.

DR PARKER: It won't make a haporth of difference. You'll never get him done.

FATHER: I'll finish Him if I have to work night and day. Then I promise you I'll turn to lighter projects. Perhaps a Virgin and Child.

DR PARKER: You'd better turn to them now, old friend, or one day we'll have you tumbling down and all we'll have to put in the auction catalogue is 'Unfinished Masterpiece'.

FATHER: They won't write Masterpiece. Not in the state He's in now. Do you suppose that girl's a virgin?

DR PARKER: Ask your son.

FATHER: I finished those pills. Give me another bottle to keep me going just for the time.

DR PARKER: We'll have to make a proper examination first. Let's leave this young lady for a while and go up-stairs, you and I, take off our shirt, lie down relaxed. [*He watches the girl all the time.*]

FATHER: You did all that last month.

DR PARKER: A month gets more and more important at the age we've reached. Don't you notice how quickly the sand runs out of an eggtimer at the end? In our prime

66

we think of a year as a thirtieth part of the life that's left, but now it's rather more than half perhaps . . . I might have to forbid you to work up there.

FATHER: It wouldn't be any good. It's all I have left – Him.

[*The* GIRL *is wandering out. She looks back and the* DOCTOR *speaks to her with his hands. She smiles and for the first time replies with her fingers before she goes.*]

What were you saying then?

Dr PARKER: That she puts a flame in my old body. [*He sighs.*] Time is short. There are things I have to finish too.

FATHER: I'm tired, Parker.

Dr PARKER: Couldn't you train your son to do the hard preliminary chiselling for you?

FATHER: If you had a son, would you let him prepare a girl for you?

Dr PARKER: You describe things so physically, my dear fellow. I only wanted a little tender unprofessional conversation . . . I should have had a daughter. It's only the young whom I love.

FATHER: Your daughter would be forty by now.

Dr PARKER: A shocking thought. In twenty years from now she would be sixty and I no older than Bertrand Russell. What a horror! Kissing her withered cheek morning and night.

FATHER: You haven't got a daughter.

[Dr PARKER *has taken up a lantern slide and is holding it to the light.*]

Dr PARKER: Who's this? Goodness gracious, it's me! And

a very good likeness too. I must say – without false pride – I don't look a day over forty. I wonder what I could have been doing with those binoculars.

FATHER: All I want from you is a bottle of pills, and all *you* do is talk about yourself.

Dr PARKER: I'm a doctor, not a chemist. I shall give you no more pills, my friend, until you let me make a proper examination. You can come to my surgery tonight.

FATHER: And sit in a queue for an hour while I might have been working?

Dr PARKER: You weren't working when I arrived.

FATHER: A man must sometimes go to the lavatory.

Dr PARKER: How are your movements by the way?

FATHER: Oh go to hell.

Dr PARKER [*offended at last*]: Not as far as that, my friend. Only as far as my surgery where perhaps we can hold a rational conversation. [*Dr PARKER gets up, brushes some dust symbolically off his brief-case and starts to leave. But he pauses and begins to make sign language.*]

FATHER: You're wasting your time. She can't see you up a flight of stairs.

Dr PARKER: I was only talking to myself.

[*Dr PARKER leaves the studio with cold dignity. A moment's pause and then the FATHER turns towards the ladder. He tests it for firmness and then begins to climb with a rope over his shoulder. A few steps up he pauses, clinging to the ladder, like a climber on a rock-face. Another step and again he pauses.*

The BOY enters. The BOY looks around.]

BOY: Father.

FATHER: Is that you, boy?

BOY: Yes, I've something to tell you.

FATHER: Where've you been? I need you. Hold the ladder.

[*The* BOY *holds the ladder with both hands and his* FATHER *begins to mount again.*]

BOY: I've been to Bentley's garage.

FATHER: You aren't holding the ladder firm.

BOY: It seems firm enough.

FATHER: Don't argue. Keep your hands on it. [*He mounts one step and pauses.*]

BOY: Have you seen my girl?

[*The* FATHER *for once attends to him if only as an excuse for not mounting higher.*]

FATHER: She was in here a moment ago talking to Dr Parker.

BOY [*almost scared*]: Talking?

FATHER: In deaf and dumb language. With the hands.

BOY: I wish I knew that language. What did Dr Parker have to tell her?

FATHER: He was amusing her. At least she smiled at him. You know what Dr Parker is. He can't keep his hands off a girl.

BOY: He touched her?

FATHER: It's too hot to slave up there today. That window's like a burning glass. [*He is seeking an excuse not to climb further.*]

BOY: She smiled? All I can do is take her to the National Film Theatre – silent pictures – Buster Keaton, Charlie Chaplin. She doesn't smile there.

FATHER: Not a bright companion.

BOY: She has a very tender heart. I used to think the movies funny before I went with her. When they threw a custard pie in someone's face or slipped on a banana skin I laughed a lot. She's changed my ideas. She's very profound, father.

FATHER: This heat would make Samson tired. My head will be better in the morning. [*The* FATHER *comes down to the floor.*] Go up and get my tools. I want to give the chisel an edge.

BOY: Father, there's something I had to tell you. About us. It's pretty urgent.

[*The* FATHER *sits moodily down. The* BOY *starts up the steps.*]

FATHER: The days are damned long without one glass of beer.

[*The* BOY *pauses on the ladder and watches his* FATHER *playing with the rope.*]

BOY: I've got an idea for that rope.

FATHER: I want to make a hand-rail round the platform. Something I can hold on to when it sways.

BOY: It won't be long enough for that.

FATHER: It was all I could find.

[*The* BOY *comes down the ladder and takes the rope from his* FATHER.]

BOY: I'll show you what you can do. You can make a loop around your waist – [*he demonstrates*] with a bow-line, and tie the other end to *him*. Under the chin – or whatever he's got instead of a chin. He's quite heavy enough to hold you if you fall. A slip knot like this. I'll do it for you – before I go away. [*He emphasizes the last phrase.*]

FATHER: Tie myself to Him? I'm tied enough already without that.

BOY: I'm going away, father. That's what I've come to tell you.

[*The* FATHER *takes the rope from his son.*]

FATHER: Parker wouldn't even give me my pills.

BOY: What's wrong, father?

FATHER: I'm tired of Him. Tired. Tired. That means I'm tired of everything. You think I own those blocks of stone? I bought them years ago in Jos. Barrow's Yard at a cheap rate because he was bankrupt. Like the man in the story who bought an old lamp at a sale and when he polished it he thought he owned the djinn who came out of the lamp. This is my djinn. He's taken everything from me, even my evening glass of beer. If I'm not careful, so Dr Parker hints, He'll take my life too. I hate Him and yet He's all I have. If I haven't worked at Him enough during the day I can't sleep, and when I've worked I wake in the morning and know that what I've done is wrong. He owns my sleep, and He poisons it with dreams. He gives me ideas and when I follow them He gives a sneer of stone – I'm wrong again. A woman who lives with a parrot grows a parrot's beak. A man becomes his work. Watch Mr Watkins of the Midland Bank when he drinks his tea. It's as though he were ladling cash with his brass scoop into a drawer – you almost hear the money chink.

BOY: I'm going away, father.

[*From somewhere outside comes the high squeal of brakes, a confusion of cries.*]

FATHER: What's that?

BOY: Only an accident in Elm Park Road. It's always happening. I'm going away, father.

FATHER: Oh yes? It's time you left. It's time you went into the world. You see I even begin to talk like Him. The world – He sent his Son there to die, didn't he? Go with my blessing and die too among the thieves and publicans.

BOY: I'm only going to work at Bentley's garage. We want to be married. Please give your consent. I love her, father.

FATHER: Emotion suits you, now I come to look at you. You have a good head.

BOY [*bitterly*]: At geography.

FATHER: I mean a head to draw or carve. The Son. After all you are a son. Before the fifteenth century the Sons were always beardless. I could have finished you in a couple of years. You don't change so quickly now. There are no contradictions in you. No mysteries. You're all of a piece. I can imagine you in wood. A bit of suffering would add a flavour – but of course you've never suffered.

BOY: Haven't I?

FATHER: You were too young when your mother ...

BOY: I'm not talking about my mother.

FATHER: I can imagine you dangling on a cross. Bony and elongated. Stuck up in one of those new cathedrals they are always building nowadays to prove to someone that they still believe. They never show the Father – He's pre-Christian. He worries them. He's incomprehensible. But the Son – He's one of us. A subject for every *petit maître*.

BOY [*whose attention has been wandering*]: It's not like her to go away like that. Where did she go?

FATHER: Who?

BOY: My girl.

FATHER: Perhaps she's exchanging thoughts with Dr Parker's fingers.

BOY: I'll go and find her.

FATHER: Better not. He might be examining her.

BOY: What do you mean? She's not ill.

[*The* BOY *turns to go, but the* FATHER *puts out his hands and holds him. The* BOY *struggles to pull away.*]

BOY: Let go of me. Father!

FATHER: There's nothing like carving a statue to harden the muscles.

BOY: Father!

[*The* FATHER *releases the* BOY.]

BOY: I'd better find her, father.

FATHER: There's plenty of time. I wasn't serious. Parker's safe in his surgery by now. Go and stand on His feet so that I can see you both. After all there's a sort of distant relationship between a father and a son.

[*The* BOY *reluctantly obeys him.*]

There's too much light. I want to get the shadows on your face. [*The* FATHER *draws the blind.*] Too dark.

[*He turns on the magic lantern. The studio is half in darkness now and the boy's face is illuminated.*]

FATHER: Now I've got the shadows right. You can imitate the lines of suffering with shadows. [*The* FATHER *takes a pad and begins to sketch.*]

BOY: They are giving me a room above Bentley's garage and eight pounds a week.

FATHER: I only want to get the bone structure in.

BOY: Bentley wants a girl to help his wife in the house, so we can both earn. I told him she was deaf and dumb. He said, 'All the better. My wife talks enough for two.' We'll be on our own.

FATHER: Of course you aren't a subject of great originality. You've been done too often dead on the cross or dead on your mother's lap like in that Pietà there. It's difficult to think of a fresh way to show you dead.

BOY: I'm pretty alive right now.

FATHER: I might put a bit of you into your Father's face. Struggling to get out. Tenderness buried even in that old Ancient of Days. Two eyes closed to everything but his own majesty, and the third eye growing, like a window on the world.

BOY: You've had trouble enough with two.

FATHER: One must guard against impatience. Another year's work won't kill me, whatever Parker says.

BOY: I haven't told her yet about the job. In case of accidents. Bentley's only got a single-bed. We'll need a double one. I thought perhaps you might lend us ... there's a double-bed in the spare room.

FATHER: Damnation. Can't you keep still? [*He tears the sheet off his pad and starts again.*]

BOY: I wanted to be a sailor once. You've seen how good I am at knots. I had dreams of ports like Valparaiso. But all I want now is a borrowed bed and a room over the petrol pumps.

FATHER: It's no good. It won't come. There's nothing in common between you and Him.

BOY: I'll arrange for old Mrs Harris to see after you. And at the weekends we'll look in too. The garage closes Sunday. I'm not deserting you, father.

FATHER: You're stupid-eyed with hope. The world is changing before your eyes. He doesn't hope. He knows. I can only carve a finished thing. No good. No good.

[*He tears off another leaf and drops it on the floor. The sound of slow footsteps on the right.* Dr PARKER *enters. He has a piece of material crushed in his left hand. One can hardly make out his features in the gloom.*]

BOY [*picking up the sketch and looking at it*]: I like it. Can I keep it?

[Dr PARKER *has come to a halt. He says nothing. A pause.*]

FATHER: What's the matter, Parker?

[*The* BOY *turns and sees his face.*]

Dr PARKER: It was nobody's fault. Nobody's. The driver had no chance. She ran out into the street as if she were blind.

BOY: Who?

Dr PARKER: It was nobody's fault. I can assure you of that.

BOY: Where's my girl?

Dr PARKER: Oh yes, your girl. I forgot. She was your girl. We laid her on the bed in the spare room.

[*The* BOY *goes past him.* Dr PARKER *tries to check him.*]
There's nothing you can do.

[*The* BOY *goes out. Pause.*]

FATHER: What happened, Parker?

Dr PARKER: She didn't suffer. If I'd known she was going to tear out of the door like that, I'd have stopped her, but she didn't say a word.

FATHER: She was dumb.

Dr PARKER: Yes, I'd forgotten that. The policeman saw it happen. He knows it was no one's fault but hers. The driver put on his brake. He sounded his horn.

FATHER: She was deaf. Why did she run out?

Dr PARKER: How would I know?

FATHER: What's that in your hand?

[Dr PARKER *looks at his hand as though he doesn't know what it contains: a piece of white material.*]

You'd better not be seen with those. Not by the boy.

Dr PARKER: I was only having a game. I meant no harm.

FATHER: She was a virgin, Parker.

Dr PARKER: How could I know that? I was being kind to her.

FATHER: You were telling her a lot of pretty things with your fingers?

Dr PARKER: How could I talk to her and hold her too? [*He sees he has made a mistake.*] Don't you throw stones, my friend. I know what happened before your last attack.

FATHER: That little slut wanted it. I did no harm.

Dr PARKER: Did your boy think that? Shall I ask him? Was she a slut to him?

FATHER: I wouldn't stay to see him again if I were you. We'd better both go out through the yard. Come to the Craven Arms. We could do with a drink.

[*During this dialogue the* BOY *enters. He carries the dead girl in his arms. He comes slowly towards the centre of the stage. The* FATHER *gives a horrified glance and backs towards the tool-shed door, then plunges through it out of sight.*]

BOY: Father!

Dr PARKER: You must excuse me. [Dr PARKER *begins to edge out.*] Patients are waiting. I'm sorry. I'm sorry that I could not do more to help.

[Dr PARKER *goes. The* BOY *has laid the* GIRL *at the foot of the statue, holding the body in his arms. The sound of a grindstone begins in the tool-shed. The* BOY *is weeping.*]

BOY: Father! She's dead. Come out of there and speak to me, father. I'm alone. I need you. Help me. I'm your son.

FATHER [*from the shed*]: I have to work.

BOY: Work! Do you know what they call you in Elm Park Road?

[*The* FATHER *does not answer.*]

BOY: I'm going away. I'm taking the first train out of here. Express. Non-stop. [*The* BOY *sees the rope and takes it. He climbs a few steps up the ladder.*] You wanted a new way to see me dead. I'll hang from God the Father's neck. Ask me not to go, father.

[*The* FATHER *comes out of the tool-shed. The* BOY *stops.*]

BOY: You are a father, aren't you? Indifference in the right eye and a bit of tenderness in the left. But you could never get round to finishing the left eye, could you?

FATHER: Why are you blaming me? I did nothing.

BOY: Nothing for me and nothing for mother. You know all about indifference, don't you, and nothing about love.

FATHER: There wasn't time for two lives with all I had to finish.

BOY: I'll finish quicker than you. [*He runs up the ladder to the catwalk.*]

FATHER: Come down from there, son.

BOY: Give me one good reason. Would you suffer or would it be a 'shocking inconvenience'?

FATHER: You've been burnt yourself. Can you blame a man who's afraid of fire? Oh yes, you can. You've the courage of ordinary folk. I haven't. It wasn't courage which made Him. You don't have to tell me how bad He is. He'll never stand in any cathedral. I haven't even the excuse of excellence.

BOY: I asked you for one word, father, but you are still talking about a bit of stone.

FATHER: This studio is a cave where I hide. With my great mudpie standing there, and my lantern slides. I'm laughable. But then I remember how they laughed at Gauguin his first week in Pont Aven. It's been a long week of laughter in Elm Park Road. [*The* FATHER *begins to break the slides.*] There go your fathers, Father Landru, Father Grand Duke and Father Davies at Brighton who killed his son with phenobarbital. And now for the Eternal Father – you'll see – I'll smash Him too.

BOY: Put the bar down. You'll only hurt yourself. Stop playing and answer me.

[*The* FATHER *drops the bar.*]

FATHER: Help me. You're my son. You're young. I'm old. I'm ashamed. I know how my conduct seems to you.

BOY: What's conduct, father?

FATHER: It wasn't all my fault. He was like the djinn of the lamp. He held me in his hands.

BOY: How could he? You never got as far as the hands.

FATHER: Please come down. Come down a little nearer. I can't even see you where you've gone.

BOY: I was proud of you. I thought you were strong. I admired you. I thought you were dedicated. I thought you'd sacrificed your life for your art. Father, who was sacrificed?

FATHER: You know a lot about me now. Pain teaches quickly. I'm frightened of pain.

BOY: I'm not. It's the only thing I have left that belongs to her.

FATHER: Come down. It's not too late for you and me . . .

BOY: Give me one true answer and I'll come. Where were you when mother died?

[*A long pause. Will it be an excuse or the truth?*]

FATHER: When your mother died I ran out of the room before the breathing stopped. I began to work. It was all I could do. [*He calls up to his son a last justification.*] I can't take life except at second-hand, but I work. I work. In dryness I work. In despair I work. As long as I work I can hold the pain of the world away from me. That's the only subject I've got – my indifference and the world's pain.

[*A long pause. The* BOY *flings down the rope.*]

BOY: Poor father.

FATHER [*inaudibly*]: No good.

BOY: What did you say, father? I can't hear you. What did you say?

FATHER: It was so beautiful standing there that first day. Waiting untouched. For the first chisel stroke. Like the world was before Adam came. But now ... now ... Look at it now. I've ruined a fine piece of stone.

[*The* BOY *is coming down the ladder.*]

FATHER: Forgive me. I've made mistakes. I'm not a clever man. And yet when I look up there ... there's something. Even if the eyes are wrong.

[*The* BOY *pauses on the last steps of the ladder and watches him.*]

It's not God the Father. I know that now. No love or tenderness there. Only pride. Like Lucifer's. Lucifer had reason to be proud. The brightest of the angels. Now he's dropped like a parachutist through the skies. Look – his feet touch the earth and he stands there, the conqueror of the world. [*He makes for the ladder.*]

BOY [*watching the obsession return with horror*]: Father!

FATHER: All I've done is not wasted. I can start again. I've got to climb up there and see him close. The ladder's firm. It wasn't vertigo. All I needed was a new idea.

CURTAIN